Copyright

Copyright 2020, Shyamali G. Perera. All rights reserved. No part of this book may be used, reproduced, transmitted or sold in whole or part in any form (print or digital) without written consent from the authors.

All art work in this book owned by Shyamali Perera. All photography credit to Shyamali Perera, Suren Weerasuriya, 123RF®, Big Stock/Shutterstock/Adobe Stock royalty free photography and the dedicated photographers at Unsplash & Pixaby.

Disclaimer

The material presented in this book is for informational purposes only. Please note that some ingredients mentioned in this book might not agree with first time users and food tasters.

CURRY & RICE

THREE GENERATIONS OF SRI LANKAN RECIPES

Recipes by Shyamali Perera

So long as men can breathe or eyes can see, So long lives this and this gives life to thee.

William Shakespeare

Dedication

To my dearest Amma on Mother's day.
The best Mom anyone could have.
Thank you for the unconditional love you
showed me, being there for me, my children
and grandchildren.

13th May 2007

INTRODUCTION

Curry & Rice is a collection of Sri Lankan recipes that have been time tested and passed down for three generations in the author's family. Sri Lankan recipes are simple to make with organic ingredients, spices, coconut milk, with no elaborate equipment required. Therefore exact measurements of condiments are deemed unnecessary for the Sri Lankan cook. The general rule of thumb is one pinch of spice is for one pound of vegetables or meat. But in many instances, there are exceptions to this rule. Hence the Sri Lankan cook puts in a pinch of this and a pinch of that and wham, bam…… the outcome is mouth-watering food layered with a multitude of flavors. The famous Sri Lankan curry refers to a variety of flavorful dishes cooked mostly with coconut milk and eaten usually with rice. The recipes in this book, written with an international audience in mind, can be altered to suit one's palate.

Have a happy and fun experience cooking Sri Lankan 'Curry & Rice'.

Table of Contents

INTRODUCTION 7

MEAT & POULTRY 10

BEEF SMORE (PAN FRIED BEEF) 12

SRI LANKAN BISTEK (BLACK PEPPER BEEF) 14

KUKUL MUS CURRY (CHICKEN CURRY) 16

BITTARA CURRY (EGG CURRY) 18

SEAFOOD 20

KAKULUWO CURRY (CRAB CURRY) 22

MALU KIRI HODI (YELLOW FISH CURRY) 25

MIRIS MALU (SPICY FISH CURRY) 26

FISH CUTLETS 28

ISSO CURRY (PRAWN/SHRIMP CURRY) 30

SALMON CURRY 32

RICE 35

FRIED RICE (SRI LANKAN STYLE) 36

CHICKEN BIRYANI 39

KAHA BUTH (YELLOW RICE) 42

CURRY POWDER 44

ROASTED CURRY POWDER 46

VEGETABLES 49

BRINJAL MOJU (EGG PLANT PICKLE) 50

KAJU CURRY (CASHEW CURRY)	53
POL SAMBOL (COCONUT SAMBAL)	54
PARIPPU CURRY (YELLOW LENTIL CURRY)	56
ALA BADUN (DEVILED POTATO)	58
WAMBATU CURRY (EGGPLANT CURRY)	60
BONCHI CURRY (GREEN BEANS CURRY)	62
HATHU CURRY (MUSHROOM CURRY)	64
MIXED VEGETABLE CURRY	66
BANDAKKA BADUN (FRIED OKRA)	68
ALU KEHEL CURRY (GREY BANANA CURRY)	70
INNALA CURRY (WILD BABY POTATO CURRY)	72
THAKKALI CURRY (TOMATO CURRY)	74
ALA KIRI HODI (YELLOW POTATO CURRY)	76
DESSERTS	**78**
RICH CAKE (SRI LANKAN FRUIT CAKE)	80
ALMOND PASTE	82
WATALAPPAN (CARDAMON SPICED COCONUT CUSTARD)	84
INTERESTING FACTS ABOUT SRI LANKA	**86**
ACKNOWLEDGMENTS	**88**
ABOUT THE AUTHOR	**89**
ABOUT THE NARRATOR	**89**

MEAT & POULTRY

BEEF SMORE (Pan Fried Beef)

Ingredients

- 1 1/2 pounds beef
- 1 pearl onion
- 3 pods garlic
- 4 slices ginger (chopped finely)
- 2 tomatoe
- 4 cloves
- 4 cardamoms
- ½ inch stem lemon grass
- 2 sprigs curry leaves
- 6 peppercorns
- 1 1/4 cup thick coconut milk
- 1 1/4 cup thin coconut milk
- 2 inch cinnamon stick
- 1 tbsp curry powder
- ½ tsp fenugreek
- ½ tsp fennel powder
- 1 tsp coriander powder
- 1 tsp chili powder
- 2 tsp paprika powde
- 1 tbsp vinegar
- ¼ cup ghee
- ½ cup coconut oil or oil of your choice
- salt to taste

Directions

1. Wash the meat and prick it on both sides with a skewer or fork. Chop the onion, garlic, ginger and tomatoes. Crush the cloves and cardamoms. Place the meat in a deep pan and pour the thin coconut milk on it.
2. Add the onion, garlic, ginger, and all the other ingredients and spices into the meat and mix well. Leave for 5 minutes to absorb the flavors. Cook on medium heat for approximately 1 hour till the coconut milk boils, simmer gently till the meat is tender. Pour-in thick coconut milk and cook for anther 15-20 minutes.
3. Pour the gravy into a bowl. Add the oil to the pan and fry the beef until browned. Pour back the gravy into the pan and stir well. Remove the meat from the pan carefully to a cutting board. Cut into slices and serve with gravy.
4. Enjoy with rice as a main meat dish or use the meat slices to make a sandwich.

SRI LANKAN BISTEK (Black Pepper Beef)

Ingredients
- 1pound rump steak
- 2 onions
- 3 pods garlic minced
- 2 slices ginger minced
- 2 boiled potatoes cubed
- ¼ cup vinegar
- ½ cup oil
- ½ cup beef stock
- 1 sprig curry leaves
- 1 inch cinnamon stick
- 1 tsp ground mustard
- 1 tsp sugar
- ½ tsp chili powder
- 1 tsp coarsely ground black pepper
- 1 tsp salt

Directions

1. Slice the beef into ½ inch slices. Make onion rings with 1 ½ onions and chop the remainder. Mix together the sliced beef, vinegar, salt and pepper in a bowl and leave to marinate for 1 hour.
2. Heat the oil in a frying pan and when hot add curry leaves, chopped onions, ginger, garlic and cinnamon stick. When fragrant add the beef and marinade.
3. Cover pan and cook over a low heat till the beef is tender. Remove the beef and set aside. Add the onion rings and potato cubes to the pan and stir fry until slightly browned. Next add the mustard, beef stock, sugar and chili powder and mix well.
4. Put back the beef slices and cook for a further 2 to 3 minutes. Serve with hot steam rice and a salad of your choice.

KU KUL MUS CURRY (Chicken Curry)

Ingredients

- 1-whole chicken cut into eight pieces
- ¼ cup thick coconut milk
- 1 onion
- 4 cloves garlic
- 2 slices ginger
- 1 tbsp curry powder(recipe on page 47)
- 1 tbsp chili powder
- ¼ tsp fenugreek
- 1 tbsp of oil
- 1 tsp of sugar
- 1/4 tsp turmeric powder
- 1 inch piece cinnamon
- ¼ inch stem lemon grass
- 1 small sprig curry leave
- salt to taste

Method

1. Mix the cut chicken with salt, chili powder, curry powder, turmeric powder and set aside to marinate. Sauté the onions, ginger, garlic, curry leaves and lemon grass.
2. Add the chicken to the sauté mix and cook on low heat. Next add cinnamon, fenugreek, sugar, coconut milk and cook till chicken is tender and well cooked. Serve with rice and any vegetable curry.

BITTARA CURRY (Egg Curry)

Ingredients

- 6 hard boiled eggs
- 1 onion chopped
- 1 large tomato cut into cubes
- 3 green chilies cut lengthwise
- 1 inch fennel stalk
- 1 sprig curry leaves
- slice green ginger chopped
- 3 pods garlic chopped
- ¼ inch piece cinnamon
- ½ cup coconut milk
- 1/4 tsp turmeric powder
- 1/4 tsp fenugreek
- 1 tbsp of chili powder
- lemon or lime juice to taste
- salt to taste

Directions

1. Mix all the ingredients with coconut milk and lime juice and cook on medium heat . Stir at all times so that the milk will not curdle.
2. Lower the heat, add the eggs and simmer till the gravy thickens.
3. Serve while hot with soft boiled rice.

SEAFOOD

KAKULUWO CURRY (Crab Curry)

Ingredients

- 3 medium size crabs
- 2 ounces shallots
- 2 green chilies
- 3 pods garlic
- 3 slices ginger
- 2 tbsp grated coconut
- 2 tsp ground rice
- ½ tsp turmeric powder
- ½ tsp fenugreek
- ½ tsp chili powder
- 1 tsp curry powder
- 1 inch cinnamon stick
- ½ inch stick of lemon grass
- 1 sprig curry leaves
- 1/4 cup coriander leaves
- 1 ¼ cup thin coconut Milk
- 1 ¼ cup thick coconut Milk
- 1 lime juice
- salt to taste

Directions

1. Place crabs in boiling water for 5 minutes, then remove and clean. Break the crab into desired portions and crush the shell a bit so the flesh can be removed easily.
2. Slice the shallots and chilies, grind garlic and ginger and grate the coconut. Place the crab in a pan and add the shallots, chilies, garlic, ginger, turmeric, fenugreek, chili powder, paprika powder, cinnamon stick, curry powder, curry leaves, coriander leaves, thin coconut milk and cook until crabs are cooked.
3. Mix the thick coconut milk with the lime juice, salt, grated coconut, ground rice and add to the pan. Stir and simmer for approximately 10 minutes before serving.

- *Note: This recipe is not for cooking live crabs*

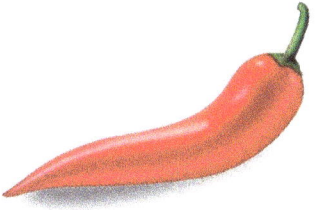

MALU KIRI HODI (Yellow Fish Curry)

Ingredients

- 1 pound fish
- 1 onion
- 2 medium tomatoes
- 4 pods garlic
- 2 cloves
- 2 cardamoms
- 1 tbsp oil
- ¼ tsp turmeric powder
- ¼ tsp chili powder
- 1 tsp paprika powder
- 1 tsp coriander powder
- 1 tsp fennel
- 1 cup coconut milk
- 1 lime juice
- 1inch stem lemon grass
- 1 inch cinnamon stick
- 1 sprig curry leaves
- salt to taste

Method

1. Cut the fish into 8 pieces or as desired. Wash well pat dry, and sprinkle with salt and turmeric and set aside. Slice the onion and tomatoes, crush the garlic and powder the cloves and cardamoms.
2. Heat the oil and when hot add the onion, garlic and curry leaves. Then add sliced tomatoes and cook for about 2 minutes.
3. Add the cinnamon stick, chili powder, paprika powder, coriander powder, fennel and cook for a few minutes.
4. Add the fish, and mix in with the coconut milk, lemon grass root, salt and continue to cook until the fish is well cooked.
5. Remove from the fire and sprinkle with lime juice when cool.

MIRIS MALU (Spicy Fish Curry)

Ingredients

- 1 pound tuna, mahi mahi or any fish that can be cut into cubes
- 1 tbsp chili powder
- 1 tbsp black pepper powder
- 2 tsp tamarind paste
- 1 tbsp of oil pinch of turmeric powder
- 4 pods of garlic
- 1 sprig curry leaves
- 1 inch cinnamon stick
- ½ cup of water
- salt to taste

Method

1. Mix the fish with all the ingredients. Add oil, water and cook on high heat till the fish is well cooked and the gravy is very thick.
2. Serve with soft boiled rice, any vegetable curry and salad.

FISH CUTLETS

Ingredients

- 1 pound potatoes boiled and mashed
- 2 cans tuna
- 1 onion chopped finely
- 6 garlic pods chopped finely
- 2 pieces of small ginger chopped finely
- 6 green chilies chopped finely
- 1 small handful each of mint and coriander leaves chopped finely
- 4 tsp of pepper powder
- ½ cup of AP flour
- 2 eggs beaten well
- salt to taste
- lime juice to taste
- ½ bottle of oil for frying
- 1/4 cup water
- 1 can breadcrumbs

Directions

1. Fry the onions, garlic, green chilies, ginger mint and coriander leaves lightly. Add the mashed potato and sauté for a few minutes. Next mash the fish and add to the mix.
2. Add salt and pepper and lemon juice and mix well. When cool make into small balls and leave in the refrigerator for ½ hour. In the meantime beat the eggs with salt, make a batter with the flour, water and mix with beaten eggs.
3. Dip the fish balls in the batter and then roll it in the breadcrumbs. Fry them in very hot oil and set aside on a paper towel for the oil to drain.

- *Notes: If the fish mixture is too soggy add some breadcrumbs to absorb the extra moisture. Do not make the make the flour batter too watery or thick and do not over crowd the oil when frying as the fish balls might break.*
- *Serve as a Snack or Starter.*

ISSO CURRY (Prawn/Shrimp Curry)

Ingredients

- 50 jumbo prawns or shrimp
- 4 pods garlic chopped
- 2 slices ginger chopped
- 1 tbsp chili powder
- 1/4 tsp turmeric powder
- 1 tbsp of oil
- ½ tsp fenugreek
- ½ inch stem lemon grass
- 2 inch cinnamon sticks
- 1 sprig curry leaves
- 1 lime- juice
- 1 cup thick coconut milk
- salt to taste

Directions

1. Wash the prawns or shrimp well and set aside to drain. Fry the onions, garlic, ginger, curry leaves, cinnamon and fenugreek.
2. Mix the coconut milk with the sautéed onions. Let boil and drop the prawns or shrimp into the gravy and cook for 5 minutes. Lastly add the lime juice and salt. Serve when simmered and prawns are tender inside.

- *Note: Please devein the shrimp or prawns before cooking.*

SALMON CURRY

Ingredients

- 1 pound salmon
- 1 onion chopped
- 1 tbsp chili powder
- 1 tbsp curry powder
- 1 tbsp pepper powder
- 1 tbsp oil
- ½ tsp fenugreek
- 2 pods garlic
- 2 slices ginger chopped
- 1 sprig curry leaves
- 1 inch stem lemon grass
- ½ inch piece cinnamon
- 1 cup coconut milk
- lime juice to taste
- salt to taste

Directions

1. Heat the oil and fry the onions, garlic, curry leaves, lemon grass, ginger and fenugreek. Pour the cup of coconut milk onto the fried ingredients and add chili powder, curry powder, pepper powder and cinnamon stick. Bring it to boil and add the fish and cook on low heat.
2. Remove from heat and add lime juice on top. Do not spoon the salmon constantly to form flakes. Serve with rice, bread or roti.
- *Note:Canned salmon can be used instead of fresh salmon.*

RICE

FRIED RICE (Sri Lankan Style)

Ingredients

- 1/2 pound of rice (1 1/4 cups)
- 1/4 cup grated carrots
- 1/4 cup leek chopped finely
- 1/4 cup white cabbage chopped finely
- 2 shallots chopped finely
- 2 cloves of garlic chopped finely
- 2 slices ginger chopped finely
- 3/4 cup organic coconut oil or vegetable oil
- 4 eggs
- 1 tablespoon ground black pepper
- salt to taste

Directions

1. Wash and drain rice and cook in Rice Cooker or on the stove top. Spoon rice well, when cooked. Next serve rice on to a rectangle dish and spread it well so the rice cools and is not sticky.
2. Heat 1/4 cup oil of your choice in a large skillet and add the chopped onions, garlic, ginger salt and stir fry till brown. Cook on medium heat and slowly add the carrots and stir fry for 5 mins till soft. Then add the finely chopped leek and cabbage and stir fry till the vegetables are transparent and glossy. Transfer to a dish and set aside to cool for a few minutes. Heat 1/4 cup oil in the same skillet and add a spoon full of rice and vegetables at a time and mix well while cooking. Lower the heat from medium to low while mixing the rice and vegetables so the mixture does not get burnt. When all the vegetables and rice is mixed remove from stove.
3. Beat the eggs, pepper and salt till the mixture is white and foamy. Heat the balance 1/4 cup of oil and make several omelettes with the egg mixture in a small fry pan. Stack the omelettes and roll them together to form a jelly roll. Cut the omelette roll in to several pieces and garnish the **Fried Rice** and serve with any curry dish of your choice.

CHICKEN BIRYANI

Ingredients

Chicken

- 1 chicken
- 2 fresh chilies
- 3 ounces onion
- 1 ounce coconut
- 3 ½ ounces fresh cashew nuts
- 1 ounce raisins
- 2 cloves
- 2 cardamoms
- 4 eggs
- ½ tsp turmeric powder
- 1 tsp paprika powder
- 1 tsp chili powder
- 3 tsp curry powder
- 1 inch cinnamon stick
- ¼ cup tomato paste
- ¼ cup yogurt
- ¼ cup oil
- ¼ cup water
- 2 sprigs curry leaves
- salt to taste

Rice

- ½ pound Basmati Rice (1 1/4 cups of raw rice)
- 3 onions
- 3 cardamoms
- 3 cloves
- ½ cup oil
- sprig curry leaves
- ½ teaspoon turmeric powder
- 2 ¼ cup chicken stock

(continued on page 40)

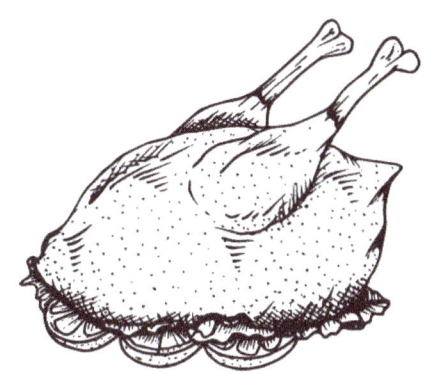

Directions

1. Wash, dry and joint the chicken. Chop the onion and chilies. Grate the coconut and finely chop half the cashew nuts. Grind the cloves and cardamoms. Boil the eggs, shell them and sprinkle with turmeric and ½ tsp salt.
2. In a blender place the coconut, the chopped nuts, cloves, cardamoms, tomato paste, yoghurt, paprika, chili powder, curry paste, cinnamon stick and remaining salt. Blend into a smooth paste then add to the chicken pieces and set aside to marinate for 10-15 minutes.
3. Heat the oil and fry onion, curry leaves and fresh chili for 3 minutes. Add the chicken pieces and fry for 5-10 minutes. Add the water to the chicken marinade, pour into the pan and simmer.
4. Meanwhile, prick the Eggs with a fork and fry in a little oil until light brown. Remove, drain and in the same oil fry the remaining nuts. When the chicken is cooked pile it into the center of a serving dish. Surround it with rice and eggs and garnish with cashew nuts and raisins.

To Prepare Rice

1. Wash and drain rice. Chop onion and crush the cardamoms and cloves. Heat the oil, and add the onion, curry Leaves and lemon grass and when fragrant add the cardamoms, cloves, cinnamon stick and turmeric. When the mixture is light brown in color, add the rice and cook for a few minutes until the rice begins to crackle. Pour in the stock and cook until the rice is soft and a bit sticky.

- *Optional: Sliced tomato and cilantro can be used to garnish the rice.*
- *Grated coconut is available at Asian grocery stores.*

KAHA BUTH (Yellow Rice)

―――――◇―――――

Ingredients

- 1 pound basmati rice (3 1/2 cups of rice)
- 3 onions
- 6 cardamoms
- 6 cloves
- 6 peppercorns
- ¼ cup ghee
- 1 cup coconut milk
- 1 sprig curry Leaves
- ½ inch stem lemon grass
- 1 inch cinnamon stick
- ½ tsp saffron powder
- salt to taste

Directions

1. Wash the rice. Slice the onions and grind the cardamoms, cloves and peppercorns together. Heat the ghee and when hot, fry the onion, curry leaves and lemon grass, until onions are browned, then add the rice and stir fry for further 3 minutes.
2. Add ground peppercorn mix, coconut milk, saffron powder, cinnamon stick salt and warm water as required and bring to boil. Cook over high heat for approximately 5 minutes, then reduce heat, cover pan and simmer until rice is cooked. Serve with any curry of your choice.

CURRY POWDER

ROASTED CURRY POWDER

Ingredients

- 1 pound salmon
- 1 onion chopped
- 1 tbsp chili powder
- 1 tbsp curry powder
- 1 tbsp pepper powder
- 1 tbsp oil
- ½ tsp fenugreek
- 2 pods garlic
- 2 slices ginger chopped
- 1 sprig curry leaves
- 1 inch stem lemon grass
- ½ inch piece cinnamon
- 1 cup coconut milk
- lime juice to taste
- salt to taste

Directions

1. Roast the coriander first on a low flame and set aside.
2. Next roast the cumin and fennel seeds.
3. Add mustard, peppercorns, fenugreek cinnamon, curry leaves, cardamons cloves and rice.
4. Lastly roast the chilies and mace. When roasted, mix all ingredients and let cool. When thoroughly cool grind in a coffee grinder to a fine powder.
5. Empty the powder into airtight bottles and store in a cool place.

- *Note: Use for cooking meat and poultry as needed.*

VEGETABLES

BRINJAL MOJU (Egg Plant Pickle)

Ingredients

- 1 pound eggplant
- 1/4 pound green pepper
- 1/4 pound shallots
- 2 pods garlic
- 3 slices ginger
- 1 cup oil
- 1 tbsp vinegar
- 1 tsp sugar
- ½ tsp turmeric powder
- 1 tsp ground mustard paste
- salt to taste

Directions

1. Slice the eggplant and green pepper lengthwise. Clean the shallots, crush the garlic and shred the ginger. Heat the oil and fry eggplant slices until browned. Remove, drain and set aside.
2. In the same oil lightly fry the green pepper and shallots and when soft, drain and set aside. Drain off half the oil and add garlic, ginger, vinegar, salt, turmeric and mustard paste to the pan and cook for 2-3 minutes.
3. Add the fried eggplant slices, green pepper and shallots and cook for a further 5 minutes. Just prior to serving stir in the sugar and salt to taste. Make sure all the ingredients are well coated before serving. Store in an airtight glass or plastic container.

KAJU CURRY (Cashew Curry)

Ingredients

- 1 pound of whole cashews
- 1 whole onion cut into cubes
- 1 tbsp of curry powder
- 1 tsp of chili powder
- ¼ tsp fenugreek
- 1/4 tsp turmeric powder
- 1 tbsp oil
- ½ inch piece cinnamon
- 1 cup thick coconut milk
- 1 sprig curry leaves
- salt to taste

Directions

1. Soak the cashews in water for half an hour. Fry the onions, curry leaves, cinnamon stick and fenugreek till fragrant. Then add curry chili, turmeric powders and salt.
2. Add the drained cashews and stir well to mix. Mix the cup of thick coconut milk with a little water and add to the cashew curry. Cook on low for 10 minutes. Serve when cashews are tender and cooked.
3. Do not make the coconut milk mixture too watery.

POL SAMBOL (Coconut Sambal)

Ingredients

- 3 cups grated coconut
- 1 onion chopped
- 6 green chilies
- 1 ½ tbsp of chili powder
- 1 ½ tbsp of pepper powder
- 1 tbsp maldive fish(optional)
- 1 whole lime-juice
- salt to taste

Directions

1. Mix all the ingredients well with the scraped coconut. Serve cold with bread or rice.
- *Note: Grated coconut is available at Asian grocery stores.*

PARIPPU CURRY (Yellow Lentil Curry)

Ingredients

- 2 cups yellow lentil soaked in water
- 1 onion chopped
- 5 pods garlic chopped
- 1 sprig curry leaves
- ¼ inch piece of cinnamon
- ½ tsp of turmeric powder
- 1 tbsp of oil
- ¼ tsp of fenugreek
- 1 tbsp of mustard seeds
- 10 dried red chilies broken into small pieces
- ½ cup coconut milk
- salt to taste

Directions

1. Sauté the onions, garlic, curry leaves, cinnamon, fenugreek and the broken chili pieces.
2. When the onion mix becomes golden in color add the mustard seeds and let them pop.
3. Then add the lentil, turmeric powder coconut milk, salt and cook on a slow fire.
4. Serve with rice when lentils are soft and mushy.

ALA BADUN (Deviled Potato)

Ingredients

- 1 pound potatoes
- 2 pounds onions cut into thick rings
- 2 sprigs curry leaves
- 1 tbsp roasted chili flake
- 1 cup oil
- lime juice to taste
- salt to taste

Directions

1. Add salt and boil the potatoes with the skin. Set aside to cool, skin the potatoes and cut them into cubes.
2. Fry the cut onions with the curry leaves and salt. When onions are fried and is turning into light brown add the potatoes with the chilies.
3. Lower the heat and cook for another 5 minutes. Lastly add the lime juice.
4. Serve with roti or freshly baked bread.

WAMBATU CURRY (Eggplant Curry)

Ingredients

- 1 pound eggplant cut into strips
- 1 onion cut into small pieces
- 2 pods chopped garlic
- 3 slices chopped ginger
- 1 sprig curry leaves
- 2 tsp of curry powder
- 2 tsp of chili powder
- 1 tsp brown sugar
- 1 tsp of vinegar
- 1 cup coconut milk
- 2 cups oil
- 1 inch stick of cinnamon
- 1 inch stick of lemon grass
- salt to taste

Directions

1. Deep fry the eggplant strips and set them on a paper towel for the oil to drain. Mix the rest of the ingredients with coconut milk and cook till the onions are cooked.
2. Next add the fried eggplant and simmer till the pieces absorb the gravy.
3. Serve when hot with rice.

BONCHI CURRY (Green Beans Curry)

Ingredients

- 1 packet of french cut beans (1 pound)
- pinch of pepper powder
- 1 onion chopped
- 1 tbs oil
- 1 tsp red chili powder
- 1 tsp curry powder
- 1/2 tsp turmeric powder
- salt to taste

Directions

1. Heat the oil and add the green beans and rest of the ingredients. Cook while mixing, until the water dries up and beans are tender.
2. Do not overcook to lose the color of the beans. Could be mixed with Maldive fish flakes if desired.

HATHU CURRY (Mushroom Curry)

Ingredients

- 1 pound mushrooms
- 1 red, green, yellow peppers
- 1 onion
- 2 pods garlic
- 3 slices ginger
- 1 tsp of curry powder
- 1 tsp of chili powder
- 1 tbsp of oil
- 1 lime- juice to taste
- salt to taste

Directions

1. Wash and cut the mushrooms, bell peppers, onions, ginger and garlic.
2. Heat the oil and add the cut ingredients and cook on very high heat for 5 minutes.
3. Then add the chili and curry powders and cook for a further 5 minutes.
4. Sprinkle the lime juice and serve when mushrooms are cooked and tender.

MIXED VEGETABLE CURRY

Ingredients

- 3 potatoes
- 2 carrots
- ½ pound green beans
- 1 small cauliflower
- 1 large red bell pepper
- 2 onions chopped
- 1 sprig curry leaves
- 3 tomatoes chopped
- 6 garlic pods
- 1 tsp of curry powder
- 1 tsp of chili powder
- 1/4 tsp of turmeric powder
- 1/4 cup chives
- 2 tbs of oil
- 1 inch stick of cinnamon
- salt to taste

Directions

1. Cut all the vegetables finely. Heat oil in a pan and add the cut garlic, chopped onions, tomatoes, cinnamon, salt and fry for about 3 minutes.
2. Add the cut vegetables and cook till the vegetables are crisp and soft. Add water if necessary.
3. Garnish with chopped chives.
4. Serve hot with rice or bread when ready.

Bandakka Badun (Fried Okra)

Ingredients

- 1 pound of okra cut into small pieces at an angle
- 1 onion
- 1 cut tomato
- 1 lime juice
- 1 sprig curry leaves
- 1 tsp chili powder
- 1 tsp of curry powder
- 1/2 tsp turmeric powder
- 1 tbs of oil
- salt to taste

Directions

1. Wash the cut okra in lime juice to take away the slime. Heat the oil, and cook the okra and the rest of the ingredients in the oil.
2. When simmered well, add salt, curry powder, chili powder, turmeric powder and cook for another 5 minutes till the okra pieces are soft.
3. Remove from fire and sprinkle lime juice.
4. Serve with hot steamed rice.

ALU KEHEL CURRY (Grey Banana Curry)

Ingredients

4 big raw grey bananas
4 onions
6 pods garlic
3 slices of ginger
¼ tsp of turmeric powder
1 tbs of curry powder
1 tsp fenugreek
1 sprig curry leaves
1 cup of coconut milk
2 cups oil to fry bananas
salt to taste

Directions

1. Skin and cut the bananas into small cubes and fry them till golden brown. Leave to drain.
2. Mix the rest of the ingredients with the coconut milk and cook till the gravy boils.
3. Add the fried bananas and simmer till the gravy turns thick and grey.
4. Serve with roti or rice.

INNALA CURRY (Wild Baby Potato Curry)

Ingredients

- 1 pound innala
- 2 big onions
- 3 pods garlic
- 1 sprig curry Leaves
- few chopped cilantro leaves
- ¼ inch piece of cinnamon
- 1 cup coconut thick milk
- 1 tsp of chili powder
- 1 tsp of curry powder
- ¼ tsp of turmeric powder
- 2 tbsp of oil
- 2 tbsp of lemon juice
- 1 tsp of fenugreek
- salt to taste

Directions

1. Boil the innala and peel the skins, and set aside. Chop the onions and garlic finely.
2. Heat oil and fry onions, garlic, curry leaves, cinnamon and fenugreek. Add the curry, chili, turmeric powders and salt to the mix and fry for a few more minutes. Then add the peeled innala and thick coconut milk to the fried ingredients and let simmer.
3. Lastly add the lemon juice, and garnish with cilantro leaves. Serve with rice, bread or roti

THAKKALI CURRY (Tomato Curry)

Ingredients

- 1 pound tomatoes
- 2 large onions
- 6 green chilies
- 1 sprig curry leaves
- 2 tbsp sugar
- 1 tbsp curry powder
- 1 tsp chili powder
- ¼ tsp of turmeric powder
- 1 cup coconut milk
- salt to taste

Directions

1. Cut all the tomatoes into big pieces. Mix all the ingredients with the coconut milk and add to the tomatoes. Cook on a slow fire till tomatoes are soft.
2. Serve with rice bread or roti when ready.

ALA KIRI HODI (Yellow Potato Curry)

Ingredients

- 1 pound potatoes cut into uniform pieces
- 6 peppercorns
- 1 onion cut into small pieces
- 1 sprig curry Leaves
- 1 inch stick of cinnamon
- 1 cup of coconut milk
- 1 tsp of fenugreek
- ¼ tsp of turmeric powder
- salt to taste

Directions

1. Cook the cut potatoes (in enough water to cover them) along with the rest of the ingredients except the coconut milk.
2. When the potatoes are cooked and soft add the coconut milk and bring to boil.
3. Add the peppercorns and salt to taste when potatoes are tender and well simmered.
4. Serve hot with rice, roti, indiappa or pittu.

DESSERTS

RICH CAKE (Sri Lankan Fruit Cake)

Ingredients

- 50 eggs
- 2 pounds rulang (semolina)
- 4 pounds soft sugar
- 2 pounds butter
- 4 pounds raisins
- 2 pounds currants
- 2 pounds candied peel
- 4 pounds cherries
- 2 pounds ginger preserve
- 2 pounds chow chow (chayote fruit mixture in sugar syrup)
- 6 pounds pumpkin preserve
- 2 pounds almonds
- 4 pounds cashew nuts
- 3 bottles vanilla essence (medium size)
- 3 bottles almond essence (medium size)
- 2 bottles rose water used for cooking (medium size)
- 2 tbsp cinnamon
- 2 tbsp cardamoms
- 2 tbsp all spice mix
- 2 tbsp grated lime rind
- 2 bottles strawberry jam (medium size)

Directions

1. Chop all the fruits & mix with the essences & leave over night. Roast the rulang (semolina) very mildly & let cool very well. When cool mix with the butter & beat it into the chopped fruits. Lastly beat the egg yolks with powdered sugar till it forms in to peaks.
2. Then mix the fruits & rulang mix in to beaten egg yolks & sugar. Fill each tray 3/4 high. Beat 10 egg whites and glaze on top. Bake in 10 lined trays (12 inch baking trays) on a very low heated oven (about F 200) till the middle of the cake is cooked (check with toothpick). Cut the cake into the desired size before serving.

(continued)

Notes

- This cake recipe is for approximately 300-350 pieces of cake, and is served at Sri Lankan weddings with almond icing(marzipan icing).
- Almond Paste vs Marzipan icing. Marzipan icing is sweeter than almond paste.
- Recommendation is to use almond paste as the fruit cake is rich and sweet.
- Almond paste recipe below is sufficient to cover one 12 inch tray of cake.
- If making the paste to cover 10 x12 inch trays, please mix the ingredients in batches.
- Store the almond paste in the fridge wrapped in plastic wrap.

ALMOND PASTE

Ingredients

1 pound almond flour or blanched almond meal
2 1/4 cups powdered sugar sifted
2 large egg whites lightly beaten
1 tsp almond extract
pinch of salt

Directions

1. Pulse all the dry ingredients in a food processor. Add the almond extract and the egg whites to the food processor and mix till a smooth paste is formed. Lightly sprinkle a board with powdered sugar to the size of 12"x12" square and roll out the paste to fit the square.
2. Gently re-roll the paste on to the rolling pin and roll it back on the unmolded cake. Smooth out any creases and cut any loose hanging edges on the sides. Cut into pieces as desired and wrap them individually in oil/wax paper.

WATALAPPAN (Cardamon Spiced Coconut Custard)

Ingredients

9 ounces jaggery (hard coconut honey)
5 eggs
1 ¼ cup thick coconut milk
¾ cup water
pinch of powdered cardamon
pinch of powdered cinnamon
pinch of powdered nutmeg
1/4 teaspoon rose essence
2 ounces cashew nuts

Directions

1. Lightly beat the eggs. Mix the jaggery and water and boil until the jaggery has melted. Allow to cool.
2. Add melted jaggery and coconut milk a little at a time to the eggs and continue to beat. Add the powdered cloves, cardamom, cinnamon, nutmeg and rose essence and pour into a greased bowl.
3. Cover with greaseproof paper and steam for 1-1 ½ hours. Sprinkle with cashew nuts before or after steaming.
4. Serve as a lunch or dinner dessert.

INTERESTING FACTS ABOUT SRI LANKA

- *Sri Lanka was a part of the ancient Asian Civilization 600 BC.*
- *The Arab and Persian traders named Sri Lanka "Serendip" for its unspoiled beaches, incredible landscape and timeless beauty.*
- *Sri Lankan National Flag is one of the oldest in the world.*
- *First country in the world to elect a female Prime Minister.*
- *Home to the world's oldest human planted tree: The Sri Maha Bodhi.*
- *Sri Lanka has the highest literacy rate in South Asia.*
- *A tooth relic of the Buddha is housed in a temple in Kandy.*
- *Volley Ball is the national sport of Sri Lanka.*
- *Sri Lanka has the best tea varieties in the world.*
- *Sri Lanka is famous for its cinnamon, coconut and precious gems.*

ACKNOWLEDGMENTS

Writing a book is harder than I thought and more rewarding than I could have ever imagined. Yet it took me 13 years to get Curry & Rice published as a paperback book. Thank you to Keerthi Meegahawatte of Southern Pacific Printing for being kind enough to volunteer his time to be the designer and printer of the 1st edition of Curry & Rice in 2007.

Also, thank you to Les Kiyuna of LSK Consulting for taking Curry & Rice to the next level by designing an eBook for me in 2014, which is available at Smashwords, Amazon, and Barnes & Noble & Ingram Sparks.

A big thank you to my present book designer Alexey Lavrentev of PhotoMagLab in Ukraine. His tireless efforts and creativity made it possible for me to publish this collection of authentic recipes as a paperback in 2020.

Above all, I'm eternally grateful for and thankful to my family: Manjula, Michael, Mikaile, Manjari, Mychal, Charith, Tracy, Ari, Suren, Diana, and Freddie. You have always given me a reason to take the next step forward.

ABOUT THE AUTHOR

Shyamali Perera was born in Sri Lanka and emigrated to the United States with her family in 1989, and lives in Southern California. While growing up she enjoyed her mother's cooking and made sure that she made most of these recipes while cooking for her family. It was important for Shyamali to have her children get used to eating authentic Sri Lanka food while living in the United States. In 2007, Shyamali published a collection of her mother's recipes as a Mother's Day gift and tribute to her mother. This book now represents a revised collection of these recipes written by Shyamali. Today three generations of the family enjoy following the recipes and cooking 'Curry and Rice'.

ABOUT THE NARRATOR

Nalini Perera was also born in Sri Lanka and emigrated to the United States with her husband in 1989. She is 87 yrs old now and lives in Southern California. Nalini has been using the recipes listed in this book for the last 66 yrs while cooking for her husband and family. She believes that using natural ingredients and cooking fresh meals enables us to live a long and healthy life. Occasionally she gives cooking lessons to her great-granddaughters who love the taste of Sri Lankan food.

www.ingramcontent.com/pod-product-compliance
Lightning Source LLC
Chambersburg PA
CBHW040752020526
44118CB00042B/2866